Jesus
Now or Never

RONALD J. FRANKLIN

Copyright © 2013, 2024 Ronald J. Franklin.

All rights reserved. No part of this book may be reproduced, stored, or transmitted by any means—whether auditory, graphic, mechanical, or electronic—without written permission of both publisher and author, except in the case of brief excerpts used in critical articles and reviews. Unauthorized reproduction of any part of this work is illegal and is punishable by law.

ISBN: 979-8-89419-076-1 (sc)
ISBN: 979-8-89419-077-8 (hc)
ISBN: 979-8-89419-078-5 (e)

Because of the dynamic nature of the Internet, any web addresses or links contained in this book may have changed since publication and may no longer be valid. The views expressed in this work are solely those of the author and do not necessarily reflect the views of the publisher, and the publisher hereby disclaims any responsibility for them.

One Galleria Blvd., Suite 1900, Metairie, LA 70001
(504) 702-6708

This book is dedicated to my Lord and Savior Jesus Christ and the work of the Ministry. Also, I dedicate this book to my children, my mother and my late father and family.

-Ronald J. Franklin

Contents

Jesus, Now Or Never Poems
By Ronald J. Franklin

Times Ahead 3
Heaven Help Us All 4
Fly Away 6
There Is No Love 7
The Last Days 8
When He Comes 10
Meditate on the Lord 11
The Need for Jesus 12
A Virtuous Woman 14
Win the Lost at Any Cost 16
The Coming of the Nuclear Holocaust 18
People Listen 20
Life 22
Song for the World 24
Love's Sweet Emotions 25
Imagine 26
The Average Sinner 28
Farewell, My Love 29
I Wonder If You Hear Me 30
I Want to Live 31
God, The Son 32

More Poems
By Ronald Franklin

We Will Rise Again 35
He Had a Dream 37
Who Can Put the Brakes on Time 38
Looking through the Bars of My Mind 40
Injustice Don't Come with Instructions 42

Acknowledgements

There have been so many relatives and friends who have been leaning posts for me as I have been engaged in completing poem after poem reflecting my spiritual journey. My mother, Annie Woodfolk, is an encourager whose faith in me has been unfailing. For her, I am truly grateful because her presence has helped to make many of my trials more bearable. My late father, James Franklin, gave meaning to being grounded in the Lord. For his support and insight for all those many years, I was wonderfully and marvelously blessed.

I have wonderful children, Brandon, Unika, Ronald, Jeren, Raven, Deven, Kalina, Jailen, and Kimora, who are just as supportive and just as understanding about my work. To them I wish to say thank you and acknowledge that their patience in and through our troubled times has been heart-warming and a source of strength for me.

I want to thank Ms. Frances Smith for her time and the advice and guidance that she has given as my editor for this work. Ms. Smith, for your hard work, please know that your reward is coming. I would like to thank and acknowledge David Altman for his "big heart", Shawn for his supportive presence, and so many others who have just been there. It's friends like you who make me *count it all joy* to look forward to each new day.

To you who through the years have read and used my poems and those who have invited me into your midst and given me opportunities to share my works with a broader audience, I am grateful. I hope this work will be a blessing to you as you read poems that address your problems or one in which you find resolution to a concern through my presentation of Christ as the answer for it. Thank you is all I can offer, but it is insufficient to truly express my heartfelt appreciation.

Ronald J. Franklin

Introduction

It has been a labor of love and spiritual growth to prepare this collection of poems to share with readers who seek a more intimate relation with Jesus. In the wee hours of the morning, I was often awakened with a poem in my head and a need to quietly sit at my table and commit it to paper. I knew then that God sought to spend time with me.

In this book of poems, I seek to share the outcome of the many hours that I spent seeking to know the mind of God and bathing in His spiritual presence. You will notice that through this work, I try to capture the essence of God's aura in the space I occupied while writing these poems. Because of the times of day that I sought to visit with God, I was conscious of the time that these poems were penned and share the information with the reader. It was an awesome experience that worked to change me and to fix and shape me for the greater service to others.

I hope that you, my readers, enjoy this work as much as I have enjoyed putting it together for you. Please share your thoughts with me – I would love to hear from you. Send me an email at sir_ron33@ yahoo.com or at this same address on Facebook.

Ronald J. Franklin

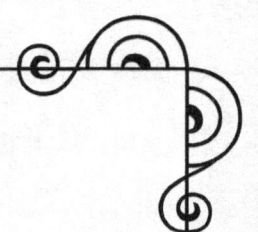

Jesus, Now Or Never
POEMS

BY RONALD J. FRANKLIN

Times Ahead

In times ahead, no longer thinking of the past,
We have all run a big race and no one came in last;
Yet striving harder to try and reach the finish line,
While pushing ahead time has matured or weakened our minds.

They say that life is a highway, and trees are all its years,
And every now and then there's a tollgate where you pay with tears.
Beyond today, tomorrow awaits,
Another chance to live in a world full of war and hate.

But in times ahead, we pray for peace, love and tranquility
Because a time and place is being prepared in Heaven for us, you see.
It's a rough road and a steep road and it stretches broad and far,
But at least it leads to a heavenly town where heavenly houses are.

As time moves ahead, we know it must go on.
So the race we run must be ran with love, joy, peace and fun.
Pay attention to these words that were said
And start living for the times ahead.

-R.J. F. 3/25/82, 12:30 A.M.

Heaven Help Us All

Heaven help the boy to find a loving home,
So on the mean streets he'll no longer have to roam.
Heaven help the family man to find a real good job
So paying his bills at home won't be so hard.

Heaven help the doctor
When he is in the sick room.
Heaven help the flowers
When they have tried to bloom.

Heaven help the mothers
When they cook, clean and scold at us.
Heaven help the fathers
When they have had a hard day, they fuss.

Heaven help the oceans
They are being polluted day by day.
Heaven help the animals
That are shot, killed or ran away.

Heaven help the junkie
Who can't leave the drugs alone.
Heaven help the runaways
That ran away from home.

Heaven help the babies
Crying in the street.
Heaven help the people
Who don't have food to eat.

Heaven help the old folks
Live to see another day.
Heaven help us all
And give us the strength to pray.

Heaven help us, so we won't fall-
Heaven help us all.

-R.J.F. 3/25/82, 1:45 A.M.

Fly Away

Often times, we have all felt the need to fly away.
In times of anger and loneliness and
When we could not find the words to say.
Even when we cannot find love in our hearts,
Try to fly away with Jesus, the perfect way to start.

When you feel the needle in your heart
No longer points to full but to "E,"
Pull over to Jesus' service station
And fill up there for free.

Sometimes we often wonder
If a place like Heaven exists so beautiful.
While living here in a world
So sinful, cold, and dull.

But as we dream one day of flying away
We should make our wrong, right with God,
And the God of peace will be with you
In easy times and hard.

When evil tries to take over,
You fall on your knees and pray,
And Jesus will give you your wings,
So you can fly away.

-R.J.F. 6/16/82 2:30 A.M.

There Is No Love

There is hardly any love found here on earth.
Gold, silver, money, to me, what is it worth?
Love is not found in the material things we live for each day.
Love is found in our feelings for each other and the way we pray.

Though time has changed the need
We have for love in life,
Yet we thank God for life
Even when it brings bitterness and strife.

Be generous, forget the past
And take the broader view;
Cast away all bitterness
And let the sunshine though.

Life is too short for grievances,
For quarrels and for tears;
What is the use of wasting
Precious days and precious years?

If God puts it in your heart
A broken heart to mend,
Remember: Love is all that will have really mattered
When life comes to an end.

-R.J.F. 6/14/82, 4:14 A.M.

The Last Days

Take a look at the day:
It's almost like the night–and saints,
We shouldn't want to lose this battle
Between wrong and right.

The unborn babies all over the world
Are dying each and every day;
And people are sick and need help,
But can't find the right way.

Wars and rumors of wars
Have spread all across the land;
That just makes you wonder,
What is to become of today's man?

And everyone is constantly
Searching for a solution;
And even the air we breathe
Has been ruined by pollution.

And tell me what can cause you more pain
Than to look down an alley
And see a junkie sticking
A needle in his vein?

There are junkies of every kind:
Some smoke, some snort, some drink–
Only to go out and rob, steal, and kill
Without taking a little time to think

Some men are without a conscience
and that's no great surprise.
The Bible said it would be so,
That's why Lord Jesus we are counting on You
To show us the way to go.

Some men have fallen weak
And turned from male to female,
And the women likewise
Have sold their souls to Hell.

The mothers are against the daughters,
And the fathers against the sons,
And the people have turned from Christ—
Even the so-called true godly ones.

The whole world is running
Blind and confused;
Even the true Christians that do good
Are being misused.

But I believe that Jesus
Will deliver us from all sin;
And please be saved when he returns,
So you can have the victory in the end.

-R.J.F. 12/1/82 5:00 A.M

When He Comes

The sky shall unfold boldly in that day.
When all who are unsaved shall be done away.
The angels shall sound the King of Kings has come.
And people will be rewarded for the good or evil they have done.

People everywhere shall see him coming through the clouds,
The ungodly will run for cover and some trampled by the crowds.
The Lord gave a warning: "Behold I come as a thief in the night."
So today everyone has a chance to make their wrongs right.

The Bible says the dead in Christ shall rise first,
And those that run from the truth shall grow worse and worse.
Those that remain will be changed in a twinkling of the eye,
But some did not live right and will be sorrowful with a cry.

God truly loves us and wants us all to be saved;
He gives us a chance to come to him, His holy Son He gave.
So give your heart to the Lord, for He truly loves you,
And when He does come back, you will rise too.
Amen.

-R.J.F. 12/1/82, 5:00 A.M.

Meditate on the Lord

Today I met a man who was lost, down and out,
Who did not know what serving the Lord was about.
I looked deep within his eyes and I saw the need inside;
I asked him a question about the Lord and he knelt and cried.

Then I said, "Look up and raise up your bowed-down head."
And then he looked up with tears in his eyes and said,
"Sir, I know I should not be sitting here feeling this way.
But I don't know the Lord and I never knew how to pray.

And I said, "Try reading the Bible and it will teach you how to live.
Then God will begin to deal with you, His Holy Spirit he'll give."
Then he said, "Thank you for giving me such strong advice,
Because no one ever told me that the Lord's followers could be so nice."

I said, "Surrender yourself to God and let Him use you as He wills.
And wait and pray for the Holy Spirit and
in due time you will be filled."
Now don't ever go around pretending that life is so hard,
But take some time out and meditate on the Lord.

-R.J.F. 8/2/83, 12:30 A.M.

The Need for Jesus

It's strange the way people ignore
The goodness of the Lord.
His blessing, His mercies, and His tender loving kindness,
All of these they disregard.

We walk around all day boasting
About the beautiful things we possess;
Riches, wealth, fame are all good,
But that's not true happiness.

We are people who spend our time repairing the things of yesterday
Instead of building for tomorrow;
And after all of our careful planning and reconstruction,
We still end up in sorrow.

But somewhere in our lives there's a turning point
For each and everyone of us,
And that turning point is to Jesus
And that's not only a need, but a must.

So tell me is it the rich or the needy
The poor or the greedy,
Who shall inherit this paradise
That God has prepared?

No, they are the do's and the don'ts
The will's and the won'ts who will
Try what very few men would dare,
And that is to serve God.

So let go of the world and all the material things
It has for the eyes to behold,
And give your life to Jesus-
And let him cleanse and sanctify your soul.

Satan sometimes makes it hard to let go
Of the things we possess with greed,
But give in to Jesus anyway, because
He is a true friend and all you will ever need.

-R.J.F. 8/22/83, 12:15 A.M.

A Virtuous Woman

Who then can find a virtuous woman?
For her price is more than gold,
Her beauty is more costly than rubies
And she's beautiful for the eyes to behold.

She looks well to her household
To make sure everything is okay,
And at morning, noon and night she gathers
The whole family together to pray.

Indeed she is so full of grace
And so full of faith,
Her husband can safely trust and rely
On her decisions without any debate.

She has an ear to listen
And she's full of understanding,
She's so kind and so sweet
And never is she demanding.

Blessed is this woman
Who is filled with God's spirit
She opens her mouth with wisdom
And everyone wants to hear it.

Her husband has full confidence in her
And truly trusts and loves his wife
Because she will do him good, not evil,
All the days of her life.

Give her the reward of her own good works
And let them praise her from within and without;
She loves God with all her heart
And in her there is no doubt.

She stretches forth her hand to the needy;
Yes, she would reach out to help a poor man,
Not to receive a reward thereof,
But because she's a virtuous woman.

-R.J.F. 1/9/84, 9:00 P.M.

Win the Lost at Any Cost

So, you say you are saved and sanctified
And life has been changed by Christ,
And nothing in this sinful world
Could make you go back to the old way of life.

You pray three times a day
And fast two times a week;
But when it comes to the lost,
Not one dying soul will seek you.

You have made a commitment to God
To do what he wants you to do.
Just look around–everywhere
There are lost souls who need you.

You would go to the ballgames and cheer
For your favorite teams to win,
While there are souls on the streets
Constantly being defeated by sin.

Therefore open your eyes and look at all
The sinful souls that are being neglected:
Then shall you see why by the Lord,
Jesus Christ, you were selected.

The Lord said "Go ye into all the world
And preach the Gospel to every creature,"
And that saying applies to each and every one of us,
Not just to the preacher.

Be strong and courageous and win
At least five souls per week,
Then shall God reward you openly
For each and every soul you seek.

Saints, the time has come to take
A stand and show Satan who's boss.
Let's go out on the highways and by ways
And win the lost at any cost.

-R.J.F. 3/13/84, 11:00 A.M.

The Coming Of The Nuclear Holocaust

The Coming of the Nuclear Holocaust
The stage is set, the soldiers are ready
And waiting for the command. While satan
impatiently awaits to turn his power
Over into the Antichrist's hands.
The whole world seems to be at a stand still
While people go about everyday life,
And those who haven't accepted Jesus as Lord and
Savior-Their hearts are filled with bitterness and strife.
Look, I could see the clouds Unfolding high in the
sky And I could see the Lord Jesus Christ
Descending from 'way up high. I could see God's people
Ascending from their graves; And I could also see people
Being caught up in the air who were saved.
Then came the great tribulation period,
Which lasted for seven long years.
And those that weren't saved-their hearts
Will begin to fail them because of their fears.
The whole world has declared a national emergency
On each and every communication source.
And the peace of God is no longer on the Earth,
Now ruled and governed by a satanic force.

A king has risen up from the East and said:
I have the answers to all the world's problems
There is a computer he'll use to brand men
With the number 666-destruction to all who
will follow him. Violence fills the air;
Destruction and miseries are everywhere.
Then there's this sudden, loud, great big explosion
Causing more damage than rust and corrosion
Its rays have spread far across the land.
It has destroyed every kind of beast and all races of man.
The Lord warned that this day would come
The pain like a woman in sorrow and travail.
People, don't let the Lord come back and catch you asleep
And you wake up and find yourself in hell.

-R.J.F. 9/28/84, 2:30 P.M.

People Listen

People, please listen before it's too late,
People, please hear me and what I have to say.

Here I sit in my lonely room,
Feeling the way a flower would that won't bloom.

But I know that there is a God
And I know that he will shine His light in my heart.

For it was His Son, Jesus, who died for our sins
And promised the world that He would return again.

So hear the message I am trying to relate
And help us get rid of this thing called hate.

Did you know that we are living in the time of the end
And have no more time to waste on sin?

So be like Moses, David, Mary and Abraham,
And open your eyes before your soul be damned.

In Jesus' name, let us serve our God
And stop living as if life is so hard;

And if you hear Jesus knocking on your door,
Open up and let Him in and please don't ever close it again.

For life is like a vapor, here today and gone tomorrow,
And if mother or father went with it, you would weep in sorrow.

I have three children to love at will,
And if God was to take them, I will love Him still.

And now my poem must end:
Tonight, say your prayers and be rid of sin.

-R.J.F. 8/1/81, 4:20 A.M.

Life

It's not enough to know what's happening
And what life is all about.
Life is a candle lit by God
For some heavenly wind to blow it out.

Life is only certain about one thing, and that's
One day life is going to come to an end.
So cling to the Lamb of Life
For in this life there is no better friend.

Life is for learning, and the purpose
Is to join up with God.
Many people know it
And still sin ten times as hard.

So Jesus, shine your light
In the hearts of all men.
And give us the strength to pray
And end it with Amen.

There is so much in life
For us to fill;
Not found in a joint, drink,
Or red or yellow pill.

Some people say that the world
Will never end;
But look at the signs, the prophets,
And the Bible, my friend.

Don't be fooled by Satan
And go around not loving, but hating.
Jesus loves us-this is true
For He died on the cross for me and you. Amen

-R.J.F. 8/11/81, 4:30 A.M.

Song for the World

A song for the world so all could see
What happened on the cross for you and me.
You've heard of a man called Jesus Christ
And heard he was pure and the giver of life;
A perfect example for all men to see,
The way we were meant to live that's you and me.

I thank you, Lord, for hearing my prayers,
I know that you hear me and know you are there.
So, people, open your eyes,
Stop all the sinning and telling the lies;
The time has come to take a stand,
Pick up your cross and follow Jesus to glory land.

The poems that I write come straight from my heart
To try and help you and show you where to start.
God said, "I am Alpha and Omega, the beginning and the end,"
And if you follow him you are sure to win.
The blessings he gives are so warm and so pure,
And if you would live His way, you will live on for sure.

Jesus is the one to call on when you are in need
Because He is a true friend and a good one indeed.
Satan will try to fool us with fame, material things and lust;
But with Jesus on our side, we have someone we can trust.

-R.J.F. 8/28/81, 3:00 A..M.

Love's Sweet Emotions

They will come when you think they are gone;
Like the beginning of rain on an early Sunday morn;
They are good to feel, but keep them under control
Because they can cause you to lose your soul.

To have deep affections for someone or something
Can show you what the joy of love can bring.
The music that you play turns on your emotions
And makes you think of all the dedications and devotions.

So if you're in love and confused
And feel as if you have been misused,
Don't give up and please don't fret,
Because the love you thought had died is not dead yet.

Love can sometimes make you feel like you want to be
Separated from it as far as the stars are from the sea;
But you know this could never be
Because we were made to love, yes, you and me.

We need love to live:
Love is the thing that teaches us how to give.
The Lord gave me a reason to love one more time
A love so free will never fly away-
We need the love of Jesus day by day.

-R.J.F. 9/2/81, 1:00 A.M.

Imagine

Imagine there is no heaven-
We will have no reason for living.
Imagine there is no love-
The kind that comes from above.

Imagine there were no children
To continue life on and on;
Imagine there were no parks
Where all can go and have fun.

Imagine there were no birds
Flying in the air,
Looking down on all things
And upon the oceans glare.

Imagine there were no mothers to cook or clean for us
And take care of us when we are sick and weak.
Imagine there were no fathers
To make sure there is enough food to eat.

Imagine all the people
Living the way God intended:
No need for fussing or fighting
And no need for sin.

Imagine no world pollution-
We could all breathe freely.
Imagine there were no aid-
To the poor, homeless, and the needy.

Imagine there was no God-
Satan would be in total control,
Imagine there were no material things
That can cause us to lose our God-given soul.

Imagine there was world peace;
We will all learn to love.
And love in the name of Jesus
With the power from above.

Imagine today was the day
For Jesus to return
Will you be ready?
Have you learned?

-R.J.F. 9/13/81, 2:30 A.M.

The Average Sinner

He comes like a thief in the night
Doing nothing good or nothing right.

He sins without thinking
And does it with a smile.
He thinks he is so cool
And thinks he has style.

He thinks he is a ladies' man
And takes them married or single.
He hangs out in nightclubs
And always tries to mingle.

He uses all kinds of bad languages and all kinds of drugs,
And calls himself a true friend;
But when your back is turned
He will stab you in it again and again.

When he shakes on a bet
He is the kind of guy who won't pay his debt
He lies and he cheats
And he never does anything kind or sweet.

He is the kind of guy that Jesus can defeat
He is the average sinner.

-R.J.F. 10/2/81, 5:30 A.M.

Farewell, My Love

Just today you told me you found another man.
It did not surprise me: I remember when I said, "You can."
At first, it did not hurt, but as the time went by–
My heart started to melt and I began to cry.

Knowing the love we once shared, you now share with someone else!
There is nothing for me to do but to say take care of yourself.
Until the end of time, remember, you will always have my heart,
And nothing could ever change that, you knew that from the start.

Many, many stories have often been told
How the new love comes and the old love goes;
My love has not gone, it is just pushed aside,
Waiting for a ticket for a second ride.

But I will try not to weep or wallow in sorrow,
I will just live for today and a better tomorrow.
So Jesus be with you in whatever you do–
I was the man for you and you never knew.

-R.J.F. 10/4/81, 3:45 A.M.

I Wonder If You Hear Me

I wonder if you hear me, Lord,
In my prayers today;
I wonder if we need you Lord,
In such a wonderful-sweet way,

Blessing me to sing this song
So everyone can sing along,
Needing love as time goes by,
Never needing to know why.

Look upon my mother, sweet Jesus,
Show her the way to carry on;
Look in on my father, Or Lord
And help him to keep up with all there is at home.

Wanting to feel the spirit, God, In our very souls;
Wanting to have you near us, Lord, in a world that is so cold-
In these times we need you more
To give us love we can endure.

Please bless all our generations
And let the world live as one big nation.
Help me find the way to love.
Give me strength, oh please.

Let me make it down the road, oh Lord,
Because love is truly in need.
The time has come for us to bend down on our knees
And to let nothing keep us from our destinies.

-R.J.F 10/7/81, 6:15 A.M.

I Want to Live

What were you thinking of when I was conceived,
Was it, *"I am going to have a baby that I don't need?"*
While you were in your pleasure, was not my name mentioned?
If not, why weren't you married or on some type of prevention?

Jesus said, "Suffer the little children to come unto me and forbid
Them not for of such is the kingdom of heaven."
And if your father and mother had made such an unwise decision,
You yourself would not be living.

Am I not entitled to have a chance to live,
Imagine how beautiful I'd have looked in a baby's crib.
There are people who would give anything to
have a baby like me in their arms,
Who would love me and care for me and smother me with their charms.

There are adoption agencies and child-seeking parents
And all kind of childcare organizations
That will help you and comfort you,
To see you through this confused situation.

You are blessed and should be happy to have a baby growing
Inside of you for nine months; but if I must die let it be
For it is not my body but my soul that God wants.
All sin but blaspheming the Holy Spirit, God will forgive.
So when the switch is turned on just remember this- I want to live.

-R.J.F. 5/7/85, 11:59 A.M.

God, The Son

God the Father and God the Son,
We have come a long way and yet we just begun.
Jesus, people often speak Your Holy name
And think what a shame you are gone.

Lord, the blessings you left behind
Lives in our souls, hearts, and minds on and on.
But you did not leave us here to burn
For Lord, we believe one day you are sure to return.

You have gone to prepare a place for us
So we will wait and pray for Your return
For in You we truly trust.

God the Father and God the Son,
Shine Your Holy Spirit throughout all the world
So all people can love and live in peace as one.

People, our lives, have moved on to great dangerous revelations;
Prophecy is nearly fulfilled, now is the time to bow our heads
And kneel and pray that our souls are saved
Before we are buried in our graves.
Amen

-R.J.F. 2/2/82, 5:00 A.M.

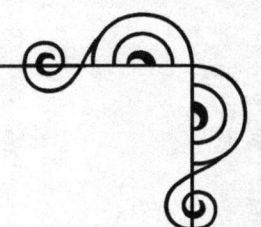

More Poems

BY RONALD FRANKLIN

We Will Rise Again

What is this? Is this a great storm brewing?
What is the government in this country planning on doing?
They say evacuate the city, But for many of New Orleans'
poor people The idea to leave does not look so pretty.

65 percent of us are people of color, But this disaster
does not exclude our white sisters and brothers. Most of
us are poor and can not afford adequate transportation.
So we will wait, starve and drown in the flood water as we
wait for our great country's transportation assistance.

I thought we were the land of the Free and the home of the
Brave? Then why did it take so long for us to be saved?
The Bible says: "The race is not given to the swift nor to the
strong", But the more I think of the way things are handled in this
country, I can't help but to see that there is something wrong.

We thank God for the people who helped, labored, and took in those
people, Donated their time and money to help rescue our people.
You have proven that though we be a country of many different
religions, We still serve our God under one big steeple.

I thought racism and partiality were things of the past?
If this is the way our country handles disasters,
Remember 9/11 and prepare for another blast.

I've looked everywhere for my daughter
And to this day, I have not seen her.
May God rest her soul, if she was taken
By the floodwaters of hurricane Katrina.

The nearby cities have filled up with people
And their populations have quickly doubled.
As we seek refuge and shelter they look at us
and say here comes trouble.

They say they will rebuild a better New Orleans
Or shall I say another City of Sin.
With all the losses and falls we have taken,
Be encouraged. God is not sleep!
We will rise again.

By: Ronald J. Franklin
12/18/05 2:44
PM Sunday

He Had a Dream

Once in a lifetime, there comes a man with
a love and burden for all mankind.
One who will die for what's right and reach out to
lend a helping hand to lead the socially blind.
One such man was Dr. Martin Luther King Jr.
who died for a cause worth fighting for.
He left a stain of peace in the hearts of all
men that the world can not ignore.
Let us not let his death be in vain.
And come out from behind the closed doors of racism and pain.
Why not make his birthday a holiday?

A man who died for world peace.
From the star wars satellite in space to the wars in the middle east.
Being a man sent by God he learned to
endure the hardships he had to suffer.
But we are all living products of the great
dream that he fought and died for.
If he had a dream then
we should have one to.
He did not do what he did for world recognition.
But it was for me and you.

Red, Yellow, Black or White we all were precious in his sight.
We have heroes who were heroes for doing all kinds of bad things.
But will not so much as remember the goodness and
accomplishments of Dr. Martin Luther King Jr.
It's time to take all the hurts, pains and indifferences
of the past and place them on the side.
And let's join together as worldwide brothers
and sisters and help keep his dream alive.

By: Ronald J. Franklin

Who Can Put the Brakes on Time

The world seems to be moving fast,
But yet no one knows where they are going.
And the people are scheming and conniving
Throwing rocks and hiding their hands
Thinking that no one can see what they are doing.
From day to day the world turns by God and God alone
And no man can stop the pace.
So I pray you are walking Holy and upright
And pure before his Holy face.
Man has created a nuclear bomb that can
destroy the entire human race
With just one push of a button.
It's time to walk straight before it's to late
And choose whose side you are on.
People very often say there is not enough hours in the day,
But if you had ten more hours
You still wouldn't give God one hour when
You fall on your knees to pray.
Men have become so indifferent and self-centered
And longer be called a true friend.
Prejudice no longer comes in black and white
But it is done in the form of paper and pen.
Children are kidnapped, raped, abused and murdered
But the world continues to ignore this matter.
They are too busy minding their own business
And sending young men off to battle.

Immorality has swept the nation from the pulpit to the white house
Proving that all men can fall short of the Glory of God,
While news reporters print tales and lies trying
to achieve good Journalism Awards
Everyday it seems to be getting worse and no
one knows what tomorrow holds for us,
It's time to receive Jesus Christ as your Lord and Savior
And in him put all your faith, hope and trust.
Man has invented all kinds of things and many others he will find
But Jesus is the one, God's only begotten Son,
who can put the brakes on time.

By: Ronald J. Franklin

Looking Through The Bars Of My Mind

Looking through the bars of my mind, trying to
break free from these chains that have me bind

As I try to channel all my thoughts and stay focused
on the lord, I can't help but to notice that my body
is still trapped behind these prison bars.

The smell and tension in this place is almost more
than I can bare, I am forced to live with and to
do things that normally I wouldn't dare.

Murders, Extortioners, drug heads and dealers have
strangely become my new friends, by looking through the
bars of my mind I pretend to ignore all their sins.

This place has the look and trimmings of a new modern
day slave system, the only thing that makes me feel free
is the fact that I know Jesus Christ has risen.

I even went downtown to the courthouse to try and find
some type of justice, deep down in the basement or shall
I say dungeon, that's exactly what I found just us.

Desperately as I look for my date out I impatiently count
every minute and every hour, having to face guards and C.O's
with attitudes who abused and misuse their power

But as I continue to look through the bars of my mind
I do know this one very thing, that God will set me
free one day and I will fly on angels wings.

                    Ronald J. Franklin
                          4/20/08
                           10pm

Injustice Don't Come with Instructions

People of the world today pretend to be blind and cannot see,
All of the corruption and injustice that's in the mist of you and me.
There are people who sit in power that won't give the poor man a break,
They are greedy of gain, always after the dollar,
They hardly give, they mostly take.
Could you believe that there are people who are
Without and who are starving in our land,
Politicians who will lie to get into an office
But when elected they won't lend a helping hand.
It seems like a man is respected by the amount of money he makes,
Even some of the preachers who preach the gospel today,
They are beginning to become fakes.
Everyday for a set amount, the court releases
Hardened criminals on out streets,
Then they look for someone to blame and point
Their fingers at us as our crime rate increases.
Everyday it gets worse and it seems there is no way to win.
A public official can openly sin and still gain the respect
Of the ungodly and some of our godly men.
When it comes to equal rights, the matter only gets worse,
They are calling men blessed who God has called cursed.
Men with men and women with women
Trying to find some type of satisfaction,
They have forsaken the way of God who
Created them to be male and female attraction.
Diseases are a major threat today and the
People are very much afraid,
Some are cancer, syphilis, herpes and
There is a deadly one called AIDS.

All kinds of drugs from foreign lands have flooded our streets,
We have gangs, gang wars, pimps, pushers and trigger happy police.
Our children are sent to school only
to learn how to become crooks,
They are no longer allowed to pray and thank
God or to read their good books.
I guess you might say that I'm a little too critical
About the way the world's system is going,
But I have a burden for all mankind and I must
Warn them of the Lord's returning.
If we would read our Bibles and pray before satan comes to test us,
Then will God give to us
The Instructions for Injustice.

By: Ronald Franklin 3/2/88

www.ingramcontent.com/pod-product-compliance
Lightning Source LLC
LaVergne TN
LVHW041556070526
838199LV00046B/2003